The little book of
explanations abo
dysthymia and lo
symptoms of dep

CW00501321

Dr James Manni
Dr Nicola Ridgeway, ClinPsyD

A product of the West Suffolk CBT Service Ltd, Angel
Corner, 8 Angel Hill, Bury St Edmunds, Suffolk, IP33
1UZ

This edition printed 2016
Copyright (c) 2016 West Suffolk CBT Service Ltd

Neither the authors nor the West Suffolk CBT Service
Ltd take responsibility for any possible consequences
from any treatment, procedure, test exercise or action
of any person reading or following the information in
this book. The publication of this book does not
constitute the practice of medicine and this book does
not attempt to replace any other instructions from
your doctor or qualified practitioner. The authors and
the West Suffolk CBT Service advise the reader to

1

check with a doctor or qualified practitioner before undertaking any course of treatment.

About the authors

Dr Nicola Ridgeway is a Consultant Clinical Psychologist and an accredited cognitive and behavioural therapist. She lectures on cognitive behaviour therapy at the University of East Anglia, Suffolk, England, and is Clinical Director of the West Suffolk CBT Service Ltd. Together with Dr James Manning she has co-authored several books on CBT.

Dr James Manning is a Consultant Clinical Psychologist and the Managing Director of the West Suffolk CBT Service. James has post-graduate qualifications in both Clinical Psychology and Counselling Psychology. He regularly offers workshops and training to clinicians throughout the United Kingdom on Cognitive Behaviour Therapy and continues to work as a practicing therapist.

By the Authors

Think About Your Thinking to Stop Depression: A Fast and Simple System to Reduce Distress.

How to Help Your Loved One Overcome Depression

Think About Your Thinking – Cognitive Behaviour Therapy Program for depression

Cognitive Behaviour Therapy for Panic Attacks: Simple explanations about the causes of anxiety, panic attacks and panic disorder with advice on how to stop panic symptoms using CBT

Upcoming books

Don't scratch that itch

How to redesign your life using contemporary CBT approaches

Cognitive Behaviour Therapy for Social Anxiety: Simple explanations about the causes of Social Anxiety with straight forward CBT approaches to help you manage anxiety symptoms and to interact in a more relaxed manner when in social environments

The little book on CBT for Depression

Simple explanations about the causes of depression, dysthymia and low mood with advice on how to stop symptoms of depression using CBT

Dr Nicola Ridgeway, ClinPsyD
Dr James Manning, ClinPsyD

Published by the West Suffolk CBT Service Limited

Registered office: Angel Corner, 8 Angel Hill, Bury St Edmunds, Suffolk, IP33 1UZ

Preface

This book was initially called "Think About Your Thinking." It started out as a therapy notes that we gave to our clients after sessions. We eventually collected these therapy notes together into a very small black book which we had printed in batches of a hundred or so at a local printers. We soon found that our clients asked for additional copies of the book for their friends and relatives. As time progressed people called us on the telephone wanting to buy copies. It seemed that every month or two we needed to call our local printers to ask them to make more copies.

To save on printing costs we eventually put the book into large scale print production. It has now been reprinted on five occasions. Each time we reprinted it we thought that it would be the last print run, but the little book appears to have a life of its own. It has proved to be popular with the public, CBT practitioners and General Practitioners alike.

The 'CBT – What it is and how it works' series

'Think About Your Thinking' was the first book in our 'CBT-What it is and how it works' series. An important question we asked ourselves before deciding to write this CBT series was – Do CBT books that are already available accurately represent what CBT has to offer right now?

The answer we arrived at was quite simply NO. Current clinical practice of CBT has developed so rapidly that it has now left behind many of the traditional approaches covered in mainstream CBT books. In addition to this, the emergence of e-books and a proliferation of e-book readers has meant that as much as two years can be knocked off the waiting time between authors writing their material and publishers making this material publically available. Effectively, this means that we can now bring you the latest information about CBT within weeks or months of it becoming available to us.

This series - "CBT- What it is and how it works"- has been designed to be constantly updated, and to demystify very common human experiences using the latest evidence-based information. We have taken many of the most popular contemporary approaches that we use in our clinical practice and transferred them to these pages to offer you an opportunity to benefit from ideas that work simply and quickly.

What makes CBT such a popular approach?

Government bodies have made large amounts of money available to complete research on CBT. This research has not only provided evidence to support the effectiveness of CBT for a variety of common conditions, but it has also made it possible for the field of CBT to attract brilliant minds from all over the world enhancing research into the field of CBT further still.

Included within a CBT paradigm we now have access to the ground breaking work of -

- British based Professors John Teasdale and Mark Williams with their outstanding research into mindfulness based CBT.
- Canadian based Psychologist Steven Hayes with Acceptance and Commitment Therapy (ACT), a new and emerging therapy that has

been incorporated into the CBT paradigm.

- British based Professor Paul Gilbert, who has recently received an OBE for his outstanding contribution to mental health. His enlightened contributions have encapsulated the benefits of a compassionate mind approach.
- Adrian Wells and his models on Generalised Anxiety Disorder and worry.

Many of the above authors have published highly readable self-help books that have offered a source of comfort to literally millions of people.

Like the above authors we want to help you by offering you practical advice within the pages of this book. We hope that you can take something away from these pages, even if it is as little as making one small change to the way that you approach things. We base this on the principle that making changes on their own do not noticeably alter your life, but collecting enough of these together will.

If you are depressed at the moment don't expect yourself to finish this book. Dip in and out of it when you feel up to it. Keep it with you to refer to it whenever you need it.

Contents

Why we wrote this book

Working clinically with individuals with depression, we searched long and hard for one really good book to lend to individuals with depression. What we found after handing out many mainstream self-help books was that over and over again most of them were either returned to us unread or with only small parts read. This occurred *despite* the valuable content of the books and the excellent qualifications of the authors.

Our clients told us that they did not have the energy or concentration to read the books. Some clients reported that the books were so large or heavy that they actually found the prospect of reading them depressing.

Reading when we are feeling depressed can often feel like a highly stressful process. This book has been written differently from others you may have read before. It has been especially constructed:

14

- To help you absorb information when your concentration is poor.

- To be kept with you wherever you go, to remind yourself of helpful information wherever and whenever you need it.

Our experience indicates that this book can be very effective when it is used to accompany therapy, and is most beneficial when individuals are experiencing mild to moderate depression.

We, the authors, love books, and appreciate that for some people self-help material alone is very beneficial. However, we also believe that self-help literature is greatly enhanced with consultations with a trained practitioner. If you believe that you are experiencing depression, we suggest where possible that you consult a suitably qualified professional for advice and treatment.

Finally, we hope that you will find the ideas within this book useful and that you

enjoy reading it as much as we have
enjoyed creating it.

Introduction

This book has been written to help you break unhelpful patterns of thinking that lead to depression.

This book is divided into 18 sessions, each of which, on average, will take no more than five minutes to read. Each session begins with a summary of its essential theme. This is then explored, in dialogue, between a Cognitive Behaviour Therapist and a client. Reflection boxes are scattered throughout the book to draw your attention to ideas of particular importance.

Session 1

The Paradox of Depression

*"Accepting your feelings is essential
to stop deterioration in your mood."*

Client: "But that makes absolutely no
sense to me at all. Why would I want to
accept that I'm feeling this way, when all I
really want is for these feelings to go
away?"

Therapist: "Well, just ask yourself, has
trying to get rid of your feelings worked so
far?"

Client: "I guess not!"

Therapist: "I'll explain what I mean. All
emotions have a function, even those that
don't feel nice (such as guilt, shame,
disgust, and sadness) and we have evolved
to have *all* of our feelings. What impact
would there be on society if nobody ever
processed painful feelings? Feeling low is

18

often connected to process of loss, or a loss of something that had the potential to happen. What would life be like if nobody experienced loss? Indeed, what would life be like if nobody experienced guilt when they had actually done something wrong? Where would the motivation for people to make positive changes come from?"

"The majority of us experience low mood for valid reasons. However, for many of us the triggers are not immediately clear. I'll explain more thoroughly why this occurs in future sessions. What I'm inviting you to consider right now though is that whatever route we take to find the triggers for our moods, we will ultimately find a good and logical reason for why we have been feeling the way that we have."

Client: "Erm? I wish it were that easy!"

Therapist: "OK. Let me put it another way. What I'm inviting you to do is quite simply to leap ahead to that point where you have found the trigger for your low mood state and welcome your low mood. I say this

because if we don't welcome our low
mood, it's likely that we will receive
multiple low mood messages that arrive
with increasing strength, until the message
is eventually hear. This will ultimately
make us feel worse."

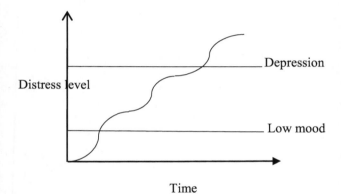

Time

*Figure 1. The effect of suppressing or
rejecting painful <u>feelings</u>*

Client: "So why does this happen?"

Therapist: "Because feelings are basic
survival mechanisms that are very intent

20

on getting their message through to us. Their purpose is to help us survive, so if we reject them they may subside in the short term, but will return later with increased strength. Basically, our feelings do this because they are trying to keep us safe, whether that is from a physical threat – For example, being physically harmed – Or from psychological threat – For example, being rejected or isolated from our familiar social group."

Client: "I mean no disrespect by this, but what you're saying makes absolutely no sense to me at all! You're saying that my feelings are trying to help me and I need to accept them, but I feel like they're trying to harm me!

Therapist: "OK! I understand that ... And, to be honest, if it made sense most people would already have found out about acceptance and they would be trying it, wouldn't they? So, given the number of people in our society who have depression, how many of these individuals are telling themselves that it's OK to feel the way that they do?"

Client: "Not many, I suppose."

Therapist: "That's right! So part of our solution lies here. When we accept our feelings, we consciously let our brains know that we have received the low mood message. This removes the necessity for the brain to continue sending low mood messages with increasing strength, and reduces the risk of our mood deteriorating. So what could you do to see if this works for you?"

Client: "I suppose I could try your idea."

Therapist: "Good for you!"

Reflection

If we interpret something in our environment as harmful or dangerous in some
way, then we come to the realisation that
there is potential for pain. This can occur
within both our:

- External environment (e.g. an
  event or the action of another
  individual);
- Internal environment (i.e. feelings,
  thoughts, physical sensations).

We naturally like to avoid pain or stop pain
from continuing. So let's use the example
of feeling low. There is nothing pleasurable
about feeling low. So if we acknowledge
and label our low feeling for what it is, it
immediately stops the brain from (a)
trying to work out why the low feeling is
there and (b) trying to stop the low feeling
from being there.

Session 2

Validate your feelings

"When we have unusual symptoms or painful feelings, many of us are left feeling confused. This confusion can be reduced by validating our feelings."

Client: "Before we go on, I wanted to tell you that your last idea of accepting my feelings did work a bit. But I'm a bit worried about discovering the trigger for my low mood ...what if I feel worse?

Therapist: "That's understandable. I'd just like to give you a bit more information so that it will make more sense."

"What I've found from talking to people over the years is that a major source of distress for people is the way that they think about their painful feelings. They often have thoughts that tend to make the problem worse. These thoughts include: "I shouldn't be feeling like this!", "What am I feeling like this for?", "Why am I feeling this?" or "Why am I thinking this, when so many people with less than me would be grateful for what I've got?"

"Asking such questions simply sends the brain into an exhausting cycle of rumination, which takes up or wastes a large amount of cognitive energy (see Session 9)."

"A more workable solution or strategy is simply to acknowledge the feeling as being there for no other reason than that it's there."

"I predict that when you do this you'll find that this takes the pressure off you, because once you believe it's right for you to feel the way that you do, you'll feel less confused. And, you'll be more able to begin taking charge of your life."

Session 3

Thoughts that don't reflect reality

"Consciousness is still not fully understood, and evidence indicates that some parts of our brain do not understand the difference between reality and fiction."

Client: "Well ... my brain definitely understands the difference!"

Therapist: "I wonder if we might consider an illustration of this point?"

"Just for a moment close your eyes."

"Now, imagine that you have a tray on your lap. Now, just imagine that there is a lemon on that tray. Next to the lemon there is a fruit knife. Look at the lemon, and pay very careful attention to its texture, colour and smell. Pay attention to

26

the shape of the lemon. Now, reach out and place one hand on the fruit and with the other hand pick up the knife. Slowly slice through the lemon with the knife. Just be aware of how the lemon juice runs on to your fingers ... and now, very carefully, pick up a small piece of lemon and slowly bring it towards your mouth ... and just place it on your tongue ... and when you've done that, open your eyes and bring your awareness back to where you are. So what did you notice when you brought the lemon up to your lips?"

Client: "My mouth started to salivate."

Therapist: "Brilliant! What do you make of the idea that your mouth had a reaction to the lemon, even though there was no lemon there? How could that be?"

Client: "That's weird ... I guess I must have made it happen because I imagined it as if it were happening."

Therapist: "Yes, exactly! You experienced that reaction because you expected it. What might that tell you about the power of your thoughts?"

Client: "That my thoughts can have a very powerful impact on my body."

Therapist: "This is the same for a lot of our thought processes. As soon as we think of an event, parts of our brain begin to activate a physiological response to it as if it were real."

Client: "So what you're saying is ... if I dwell on negative things happening in my life, I'll start to feel depressed."

Therapist: "Exactly! When we think about or visualize painful events our bodies create a parallel physiological reaction matching the thought. This is why thinking about painful thoughts can bring about very intense feelings."

Session 4

Why the brain struggles
With negatives

*Be mindful when thinking about what we
don't want to happen in our lives. Our
brains use considerable resources
engaging in this type of information
processing.*

Client: "OK ... But what has this got to do
with how I'm feeling?"

Therapist: "I appreciate that the idea may
sound unfamiliar. However, in order to
block thoughts that we don't want, our
brain has to complete several activities.
The first thing it needs to do is think about
what you don't want, so that it knows what
it should *not* be thinking about."

Client: "This is going from bad to worse!"

Therapist: "Consider this...Whatever you do now, it is very important not to think of a pink elephant smoking a pipe. Whatever you do, do not under any circumstances let that image come into your mind. OK? Now when I said that what was the first thing that came into your mind?"

Client: "A fleeting image of a pink elephant ... I must say ... That's really weird!"

Therapist: "Now what do you think would happen if you kept telling your mind not to give you the image of the pink elephant smoking a pipe?"

Client: "Would it come back even more?"

Therapist: "Yes! That's exactly what happens. ... What happens after that is even more interesting. Parts of our brain spend huge amounts of resources trying to stop the very idea that we don't want to think about from coming into conscious awareness. And then, when we get tired and stressed, those parts of our brain become compromised and less able to block thoughts and – hey presto! – We gain access to the thought that we don't want."

Client: "I think that actually might make some sense. Is that why I have more distressing thoughts when I'm tired?"

Therapist: "That's right! So a key point to remember here is that our brain finds thinking about what we *want* to happen much easier than thinking about what we *don't* want to happen."

Reflection

Feeling distressed and defeated can result in us trying to control something that cannot be controlled.

In this respect, a problem can occur if we believe that we should be in control of the thoughts in our head or that we should be able to control our feelings. Now, because a controlling strategy generally does not work very well, we can find that we blame ourselves, thinking that there is something wrong with us that needs fixing. When we are depressed, we then focus and ruminate on why we are depressed. This in turn makes us feel more dejected, helpless and hopeless.

To counteract the above, new strategies that work have to be introduced. This way we can prevent a suffering process (associated with feeling depressed) and replace it by responding more adaptively to the initial thoughts and feelings that we notice.

Session 5

Teach Your Brain That a Thought is Just a Thought

"When we tell ourselves that we are just having a thought about a distressing event, our distress levels reduce."

Client: "But surely I know that I'm having a thought?"

Therapist: "There is a big difference between noticing and telling ourselves that we're having a distressing thought and being in the distressing thought."

Client: "Can you elaborate?"

Therapist: "OK. Think of a distressing thought, maybe about your depression, getting so bad that you're no longer able to function. You lose your job and your family. You end up alone, isolated, and rejected."

"Immerse yourself in that thought."

"Now, how do you feel?"

Client: "Terrible, my stomach is turning over ... I feel as though I can't breathe."

Therapist: "OK. Now I want you to do something slightly different. I just want you to tell yourself the following: "I am aware that I am having a thought about my depression getting so bad ... and so on". ... Now what happens when you do that?"

Client: "It's strange. It's as if the pain is floating away...It's hugely relieving!"

Therapist: "So how does that happen?"

Client: "I don't really know, but there's definitely something in it. Could it be that I'm helping my brain to understand that the thought is not actually happening, and all that's really happening is that I'm having a thought?"

Therapist: "Yes! You've just used your awareness to acknowledge that you've had a thought or a series of thoughts. And, these thoughts are indeed just thoughts and not imminent facts relating to you and your immediate environment."

Session 6

Be Mindful of the Questions You Ask Yourself

"The questions that we ask ourselves drive the mental processes in which our brains engage. It is very important, therefore, to think carefully about what we want to achieve, before we decide which questions to ask."

Client: "I'm beginning to see how my thoughts influence my mood to some extent, but how do questions affect anything?"

Therapist: "Let's consider this. When was the last time that you asked yourself a question and your brain turned round and told you it couldn't be bothered giving you an answer?"

Client: "Well ... I think ... Never."

Therapist: "OK. So let's make our starting point there. Whenever we ask ourselves a question, our brain is compelled to answer. Our brain instigates a search process and comes up with an answer based on all the information available. So what do you think it would come up with if you asked it, "Why does this always happen to me? What's wrong with me?"

Client: "Erm ... That ... I'm useless ... That I'm somehow defective ..."

Therapist: "And what else will it come up with?"

Client: "Memories from my past, teachers at school, failing an exam ... Anything, I suppose, that says I'm useless."

Therapist: "And, when you've accessed all of those thoughts, how does that leave you feeling?"

Client: "Terrible, awful, really bad."

Therapist: "And, in terms of answering your question, how would you rate your brain's performance, in accessing that material?"

Client: "I guess it's done really well."

Therapist: "So based on what we've just talked about, would you say that your brain is trying to undermine you?"

Client: "No ... it's not trying to undermine me. Even though I don't like the answers, I suppose it's just doing what I asked of it ..."

Therapist: "So what would happen if you asked *different* questions?"

Client: "Maybe it would come up with different answers."

Therapist: "Exactly! So taking charge of the questions that we ask ourselves is essential if we want to decide how we think and feel.

Reflection

Note well that the use of a question beginning with the word "Why" when applied to the self should always be used with great caution!

Session 7

Ask Questions That Help You Thrive

"The questions we ask ourselves are essential in setting the course and direction of our lives. Used wisely, the right questions can help us achieve great things."

Client: "So how do I know what questions I should ask? I didn't realise this was all so complicated!"

Therapist: "Well, it's simpler than most people realise. Before we ask questions of ourselves we need to know what we actually want."

"Place an image of something that you think is reasonably hard to achieve in your mind, and quite simply tell your brain that you want it to happen."

Client: "Is that it?"

Therapist: "That's just our starting point. Lots of people put images of what they want in their mind and nothing happens. The real impact of making things happen is with the use of questions. Let's test it. Hold an image of what you want to happen in your mind and keep asking your brain, "What am I going to do to make that happen?" Then every time your brain gives you an answer ask yourself, "and what else am I going to do to make that happen?" You'll find that within a short space of time, your brain will start to give you answers. Just try it!"

Client: "OK. Just to recap, what I really want is to be happy in my relationship. ... So I'm putting an image of that into my mind, and I'm asking myself, "What am I going to do to make that happen?"

...[a minute passes] ...

"That's really weird. My brain's just told me that I should listen more, and make more little gestures ... That's amazing! I didn't realise it could do that. I feel like I've just got a new toy!"

Therapist: "Fantastic, isn't it? Now, let's take it further. When solutions come up, I want you to choose the solutions that you like and follow the same procedure again – Visualise and use the same questions."

Client: "OK"
            ...[a minute passes] ...

"That's fascinating! My brain has just told me to put a lot of thought into what my partner really likes."

Therapist: "OK, let's recap. Our brain thrives when we ask it "How" and "What." All we need to do is ask."

Reflection

We can maintain the direction we want in our lives by visualising what we want and follow that by asking "how" and "what" questions.

Session 8

Beware of Thinking Errors

"When we experience depression our thinking style tends to change. This change in thinking style can distort our perception, mood and behaviour. It is vital to recognise when these processes are occurring, so that we can detach from them."

"How could anyone think that this department is under staffed?"

Client: "This seems a bit frightening – I didn't realise that these kinds of things happened. Are you trying to tell me that my thoughts aren't real?"

Therapist: "Well, your thoughts are real, just altered. Basically what I'm suggesting is that our thinking can move from being adult – And, by that I mean quite balanced, flexible, expansive, considering, methodological, and with shades of grey – To a more rigid style, not dissimilar to that of children. We can start to think in black and white terms and think in terms of all, nothing and everything. Basically our thinking can become quite rigid."

Client: "So what do I do then?"

Therapist: "I'm glad you asked that. This is the time to start practising the exercise that we talked about in Session 5. Just start labelling your thinking style. For example, "I'm recognising that I'm having a thought that people always treat me this way" and/or "I'm recognising that I'm having a thought that nothing I ever do turns out right."

Client: "So what will this do?"

Therapist: "When we do this, instead of being in our thoughts and being highly influenced by them, we will instead have an awareness of our thinking style and we will be less likely to be drawn into further distorted patterns of thinking."

"If we're drawn into distorted thinking patterns, we will be more likely to engage in unhelpful coping strategies. After all, if we think things are never going to work out, what would be the point in trying to do anything?"

"Remember that we only use unhelpful coping strategies – For example, avoiding problems– When we believe that the thoughts that we have are true. Seeing the thoughts for what they are – Just ideas – Immediately changes our relationship with our thoughts. Changing our relationship to the thoughts instantly changes the believability of our thoughts and then we can start to feel better."

Reflection

The moment we say to ourselves "Nothing ever works for me", "He/she always does that to me" or "I'm never considered," this will be our reality at that moment in time.

If it were in fact true that nothing ever worked out, that all people always behave like this to us, all of the time, and that we were never considered, that indeed would be pretty depressing!

Awareness, without judgement, of our thinking style allows us to quickly acknowledge obvious distortions. This acknowledgement alone has a marked positive impact on our emotions. We will be more able to stand back from seeing the "alls" and "everythings" as facts and notice them instead as a thinking style.

Session 9

Decide to Stop Ruminating

"Rumination refers to persistent reflection and brooding on a problem. Ruminating about why you are depressed will not improve your mood."

"I recommend you spend less time in your cubicle."

Client: "So how do I stop myself from ruminating?"

Therapist: "I'm very happy that you asked that. The first stage is the process of detachment – And, to detach we need to decide that we want to stop ruminating. I think it may be helpful to explain how this works in a bit more detail."

"If we look at rumination as a problem-solving process that we use to help ourselves feel better, when was the last time it worked to make things better for you?"
Client: "Well, to be honest I can't remember a time when it ever made me feel better."

Therapist: "So, how about if you ruminated or dwelled on things more ... Would it work then?"

Client: "No ..."

Therapist: "So what would you do, let's say, with something in your house that doesn't work any more?"

Client: "Throw it out, I guess ... But it's not as simple as that for me. My rumination works automatically, I haven't got any choice."

Therapist: "We'll talk about that in our next session. All we need to do at this stage is to make a decision to consider a different strategy to that of ruminating or dwelling on things. Remember that rumination usually leaves us feeling much worse."

Reflection

Rumination could be regarded as potentially useful as a problem-solving strategy, as it helps us to generate lots of possibilities, and can be helpful when there is a tangible problem to be solved. However, when we ruminate to help us understand why we feel bad, we will simply be guided to the potential evidence that supports why we feel so bad. This way we will ultimately solve nothing and only confirm our worst fears, for example, that there may be something wrong, defective, bad about us, after all. This, of course, leaves us feeling terrible and pretty much despairing and despondent.

Session 10

Detach Yourself from Ruminative Cycles

"Rumination does not work automatically. It requires an element of conscious choice. Detach from it."

Client: "I'm listening ... But I can't understand how it's not automatic."

Therapist: "OK. I'll explain what I mean by drawing a diagram for you (figure 2). Now, when you look at the diagram you'll notice that there's a large box, and I've labelled that Box A. Let's imagine that Box A is devoted to our conscious awareness. So, in other words, Box A determines what we are currently aware of at any point in time."

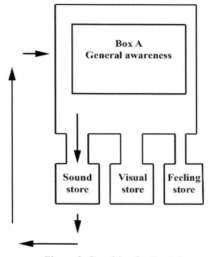

Figure 2. Cognitive feedback loop

"I'm going to take this even further and suggest that Box A has Attention Deficit Disorder. In other words any information

54

that comes into this part of the brain quickly fades and doesn't stay there for very long."

Client: "So we need to do something to keep it there?"

Therapist: "Exactly! Information in Box A passes through and fades so quickly, (and information goes in and out of Box A so quickly), that there are certain things that the brain needs to do to remember what it's thinking about."

"If we look at the diagram again you'll see that underneath Box A are some smaller boxes, and I've called these cognitive stores. One store is for visual images, another is for sound, and the third is for feelings. The stores can only keep hold of very limited amounts of information. To give you an example, let's think of the sound store where verbal thoughts are held."

"Now to give you an explanation about the capacity of the sound store: If I presented you with 9 random digits, how many do you think you could remember?"

Client: "I don't know, 5 or 6 maybe!"

Therapist: "So what do you make of that?"

Client: "I guess that's not very many."

Therapist: "It's the same for most of us. On average the majority of us can only remember between 5 and 8 randomly presented verbal units of information. For most of us 9 digits is beyond the capacity of the sound store. In this respect, the capacity of the sound store is very limited. Does this make any sense so far?"

Client: "I'm not sure ..."

Therapist: "Well I'll go on a bit further and then we'll see if things are clearer. Now, in order to keep things alive in awareness

(Box A), the brain needs to keep information briefly in its sound, visual or feeling stores and then feed it back into general awareness. To do this it uses a looping mechanism. Basically, using the looping mechanism is the only way that the brain can register what it's supposed to be thinking about. To demonstrate this, I'd just like us to work through an exercise, and be aware of what we've just talked about."

Client: "OK."

Therapist: "I want you to close your eyes for one minute, and just pick out a problem that has bothered you a lot recently. When you've done that let me know."

Client: "OK ... I think I said something on the telephone the other day that upset a friend, and she still hasn't phoned me back."

Therapist: "Right! Now we're going to use this problem to ruminate, primarily using the sound store. I want you to loop information through your sound store by asking yourself lots of questions about the telephone call. If images come into your mind, ask yourself questions about them such as, "What does this image mean about me?" I just want you to be aware of the conscious processes involved in rumination."

... [one minute passes] ...

"OK, now how was that for you? How do you feel?"

Client: "Pretty terrible."

Therapist: "OK, so that's what we expected. It feels familiar, right? ... Now I'd like us to try something slightly different. Just close your eyes for one minute and for every thought you have in this minute simply label it as you did in

58

Session 5. Hear yourself say, "I am recognizing that I'm having a thought about ... I recognize that I'm having an image of ... I recognize that I'm feeling a sensation of ...", And then just let it go in its own time. By doing this, you're not going to consciously put this information in the loops. You don't need to try to let it go. Just label and recognize what you experience and allow it to pass on by. The thought will fade all by itself."

"I'll let you know when a minute is up."

... [a minute passes] ...

"OK. Let's think about what you noticed."

Client: "Well ... That was quite amazing. It felt like a relief ... I started to feel more relaxed."

Therapist: "What do you make of that?"

Client: "I'm not sure ... But ... It seems that at last ... It feels as though I've actually got a strategy that I can use."

Therapist: "And, knowing you can use this strategy, how does that make you feel?"

Client: "Really good, although a bit apprehensive.

Therapist: "Of course you are. This is genuinely new to you. Now, the important thing to think about here is that rumination is a conscious choice. And, because it is a conscious choice you can freely detach from it."

Reflection

Would you listen to, or follow the advice of someone who wanted to help you, but whom you considered to be poorly informed, ignorant, or intellectually undeveloped?

How would you respond to them if they said things to you such as, "You're an idiot" or, "You're stupid"?

An educated guess would be that you would listen to them with compassion, let them have their viewpoint, and then quietly choose to follow your own advice.

Just ask yourself what might be the best way to respond to that critical part of you – a part that is actually trying to be helpful, but doing it in an ineffectual way.

Be aware of how you respond to your inner critic ... Or it could well end up managing you.

Session 11

Take Action!

"Consider changing your behaviour, or if you cannot change your behaviour, consider altering your perception of your situation. Either way – Take action!"

Client: "But, my behaviour isn't the problem – If I wasn't depressed, my life would be fine!"

Therapist: "An interesting idea, yet low mood could be viewed simply as a signal that something needs to change. So why shoot the messenger?"

Client: "I'm not sure I get you ..."

Therapist: "Our experience of low mood is a general physiological and emotional response that's often connected to the meaning that we're taking from a situation."

"One reason why our mood may become low is because our basic rules for how we expect to live our lives, or expect others to treat us, are being continually violated. Let's imagine that I have a rule that "Others must listen to me, value me, and treat me with respect at all times and then I will be OK.""

Client: "Sounds like me ..."

Therapist: "So let's imagine that I kept putting myself in a situation where others didn't comply with that rule. Let's say I put myself in a relationship with a dismissive individual who listened to only half of what I said – how would I feel?"

Client: "Exasperated, I guess."

Therapist: "What if I then told myself that I shouldn't be feeling exasperated and I kept going back, hoping that one day the dismissive individual would start listening to me and respecting me. Yet they never did. How I would feel then?"

Client: "Depressed, despondent ... and pretty hopeless."

Therapist: "Exactly! Now in this example, we have a choice. We can either take ourselves away from this position. We can maybe surround ourselves with people who comply with our rules. Maybe we can quite simply change the rules or make the rules more flexible. For example, we could change the rule to "Others may treat me disrespectfully from time to time, but their behaviour is not related to my value. In fact, their behaviour probably says a lot more about them.""

"Either way, action is required. So a key issue to decide is: are my rules reasonable, and, if they are, do I want to change my situation? Or is staying in my situation more important to me, and, in that case, do I need to change my rules?"

Session 12

Why we have rules

"Rules are the protection strategies that our brains develop early in life to make sense of the world. They are generally developed by our minds to help keep us safe from perceived physical or psychological danger."

Client: "So the rule 'If people are kind to me and treat me with respect at all times, then I will be OK' is protective ... I don't understand! In our last session I thought you said this rule can cause low mood."

Therapist: "Yes, our rules can lead to us feeling depressed if they're challenged or violated for prolonged periods. But what we need to remember is that for the majority of us the intention behind the rule being developed in the first place was to protect us, to help us make sense of our relationship with others in the world."

Client: "I don't understand."

Therapist: "Let's imagine that there's a small child, let's say a five-year-old boy or girl, and that child doesn't see his or her father or mother very often. For simplicity, can you just pick for me a boy or a girl, and a parent, either mother or father."

Client: "OK, a boy and his father."

Therapist: "Good. Now we'll add to that. Let's say that when the father is around, he doesn't interact with his son very often. Now, how might a five-year-old child make sense of his father's behaviour?"

Client: "Perhaps he thinks the father has other things to do?"

Therapist: "Let's remember that this is a five-year-old boy and because his brain is still growing and developing, he may have more difficulty thinking about how others might be thinking or feeling. Instead, what he's much more likely to do is to think egocentrically."

Client: "Egocentrically?"

Therapist: "By that I mean that the boy would be more likely to put himself in the centre of his world. In other words he would be more likely to think that things happened because of him and if things went wrong, blame himself and see himself as wrong, at fault or indeed faulty in some way. He's much less likely to link his father's behaviour to his father being stressed or having psychological problems, or whatever."

"My experience tells me that this is the case because, when I've met children in exactly this position, they've said things like, "If only I could be different, then maybe Dad would spend more time with me." And, what do you think this could lead to if the child continues to feel this way?"

Client: "Will the child start acting in a different way?"

Therapist: "Yes. Maybe the child will try out different strategies to find out what will get Dad's attention. Maybe he'll play up. Maybe he'll find out that if he's compliant, or if he tries to please his father, then his father reacts to him in a different way. Or maybe no matter what the child does, the father continues to be distant and neglectful. What meaning might the child take from that?"

Client: "That there really is something wrong with him and that he isn't lovable?"

Therapist: "Yes"

Client: "That's really sad."

Therapist: "Yes, and it's sad because we know that the child isn't unlovable. That's simply not accurate."

Client: "So what if the child learns that if he changes his behaviour people will be nice to him? But doesn't everybody do that?"

Therapist: "Well, a lot do. Let's consider, if a child feels that he needs to change his nature to keep others happy, what will he start to believe about who he truly is?"

Client: "That he's unlovable as he is, or that he's unacceptable in some way."

Therapist: "That's exactly what he'll think – And then this will become like a painful secret that he keeps to himself and, as time goes by he gets better and better at keeping others happy. Maybe he does really well at school or maybe he's funny and entertaining – Or maybe he's quiet and stays in the background. And, while all

this is going on he may feel lost – Thinking
that nobody really knows him. Maybe
when others upset him or act in an
offensive manner, he may keep his feelings
to himself – so others will never really
know how he feels. All of the time he holds
back because he doesn't want others to
know that he's not good enough, or that
there's something wrong with him. I'll
show you what I mean ..."

"Now this diagram (figure 3, *overleaf*)
shows the hypothetical situation. We have
the beliefs as you suggested – "I'm
unlovable" and maybe "I'm unacceptable"
– and we know that the child learns to
believe these things as a result of another
individual's interactions with him, in this
case his father. He then learns what he
needs to do – In this case it's to keep
others happy – And there are a variety of
things that he does to make this happen.
Now the essence of the protection is that
the child believes he's keeping himself safe

by keeping others happy! Are you with me so far?"

Client: "Yes, I think so. The child is frightened that other people will see him for what he thinks he really is – Unlovable or unacceptable – So he thinks that if he behaves in certain ways then he'll be OK."

Therapist: "That's right ... And then how do you think he'd feel if one day, when he was older, he found out that he had to tell someone something that would make them feel upset or uncomfortable?"

Client: "He wouldn't want to do it?"

Therapist: "Why?"

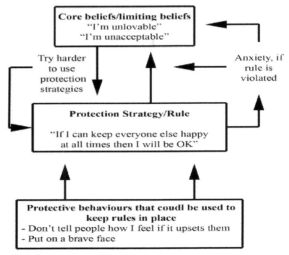

Figure 3. Reinforcement of limiting beliefs.

Client: "It would probably make him feel anxious."

Therapist: "That's right! So telling someone something that they didn't want to hear could be a big threat to him — And normally when people become anxious, the first thing that they try to do is to compensate even more. So in this case the boy would try even harder to keep others happy."

Reflection

Rules are developed by our brains to keep us safe. If they are developed early in life in a maladaptive environment, they may help us during that period of time. However, as soon as we grow older and move into a more adaptive environment, the rules can quickly become rigid and therefore unhelpful.

Session 13

Identifying Your Own Limiting Beliefs

"It is very important to know what limiting beliefs we may have. If we don't, there is a high probability that rules and expectations connected to them will be running our lives without us even realising it."

Client: "So how do I find out what my limiting beliefs are?"

Therapist: "The first thing I'd like to let you know is that accessing limiting beliefs may well make you feel uncomfortable. This discomfort will be there only if you currently believe your limiting beliefs are facts or they're fixed truths about you."

"Despite the discomfort, accessing these beliefs will mark the beginning of disempowering them."

Client: "Well, if it would help, I'm willing to try anything."

Therapist: "OK ... What I'd like you to do is just think of a recent situation – Maybe an event that you experienced over the last month – Where you behaved in a way which on reflection may have been an overreaction to a situation ..."

Client: "... Right, I've thought of one."

Therapist: "Now, I'd like you to put yourself back in that situation as best you can. Just think of the thoughts you had back then ... and now concentrate on one of the more distressing thoughts."

Client: "OK, I'm thinking of one ... That I'd said something that had been really upsetting to a friend of mine."

Therapist: "OK. Now stay with that thought, paying particular attention to how you're feeling when you have that thought, and to what that experience feels like in your body. Now, how are you feeling?"

Client: "Pretty tight in my chest and in my arms."

Therapist: "OK. That's what we're looking for. I just want you to stay with that feeling while you think about the following questions. Now still focussing on that feeling ... If that thought were true – That your friend really had been upset by something that you'd said – What do you think that might mean about you?"

Client: "It could mean that I wasn't a very good friend."

Therapist: "Now that's useful. Still concentrating on that feeling in your chest and in your arms ... If that were true – That in fact you weren't a good friend –

What would that say about you?"

Client: "But no! There have been lots of times when I have been a good friend – And surely my friend wouldn't harbour too much ill feeling?"

Therapist: "OK. Now we're going into logic! The feeling is saying something else! Focus on the feeling – What does the feeling say? If you weren't a good friend what might that mean about you?"

Client: "… That I'm … Not … A very nice person."

Therapist: "Well done, you've got there. I know that was very hard for you! So what would be so bad about not being a very nice person?"

Client: "Nobody would like me. I'd be all alone with no friends and lonely … But I know that wouldn't happen – I know that

I'm a nice person. I've got lots of friends. People like me ..."

Therapist: "Exactly! You know you're a nice person! What we're dealing with here though isn't an idea based on facts or evidence. In fact, I'm willing to bet that you'll bend over backwards to keep people happy – And to be viewed as not a nice person is the last thing that you'd want."

Client: "Yes! You're right!"

Therapist: "Right, so have you ever wondered how much choice you have in the way that you think or behave?"

Client: "What do you mean – Choice?"

Therapist: "Well, I'll explain further in our next Session. We'll start with a working hypothesis that you have an underlying belief that you're not a nice person. A key thing to identify here is that when you feel that you have to behave in a certain way, for example, bending over backwards to keep others happy, you may be compensating for limiting beliefs which are influencing your life without you realising it."

Session 14

Disempowering Limiting Beliefs

"Once limiting beliefs are uncovered, it is very important that we do everything in our power to destabilise them. If we don't we can expect to receive regular doses of distress."

Client: "So what can I do to destabilise my limiting beliefs?"

Therapist: "Let's start right at the beginning. Let's go right back – Right back to the time of your birth. Now when you were born, imagine yourself being held by an adult – maybe your mother, your father, or someone else present at the birth. Perhaps your eyes were open and you were looking around, or maybe you were absorbing the shapes and figures in this new environment. Were you born believing that you were not a nice person?"

Client: "No!"

Therapist: "So where did you learn to believe it?"

Client: "I've never thought about that before ... I don't know."

Therapist: "So we know that you weren't born believing it. So where do you think people normally learn to believe these types of ideas?"

Client: "From their parents, I suppose."

Therapist: "So would you agree that perhaps limiting beliefs are ideas about the self that are taught by others and are not part of people's genetic make-up?"

Client: "I guess so."

Therapist: "Now, I'd like to ask you a question ...What would happen if deep down inside yourself you felt that you were fundamentally OK? What would happen to your protection strategy of trying to keep other people happy at all times?"

Client: "I wouldn't need it, I suppose."

Therapist: "And, if this were the case – That you didn't need to use your protection strategy – What would your life be like?"

Client: "Life would be much easier!"

Therapist: "How would that feel?"

Client: "Liberating!"

Therapist: "So now what we need to do is to regularly bring your thoughts into conscious awareness and assess whether limiting beliefs are in operation. If they are, ask yourself: "Where did these beliefs come from?", "Who taught me these beliefs?", "Do these beliefs really say more about the people who taught me them?", "How familiar are these beliefs?", "How old are these beliefs?", "What age was I when I learnt these beliefs?" and "If I could choose right now today to have a belief, is this a belief that I would choose?" These questions will begin the process of destabilising your limiting beliefs."

Session 15

Change Your Reinforcement Cycles

"Limiting beliefs have a tendency to reinforce themselves. In this respect the more that we attempt to protect ourselves from our feared beliefs, the more likely it is that they will be reinforced. This reinforcement inevitably empowers our limiting beliefs still further. It is important, therefore, to consider dropping our maladaptive protection strategies."

Client: "So what you're saying is that if I use my protection strategies to stop my limiting beliefs from being true then it's more likely that I'll believe my limiting beliefs. Surely that doesn't make sense – Wouldn't the opposite, in fact, happen?"

Therapist: "Well, let's look at what we discussed in Session 14. I'll draw another diagram for you." (See figure 4.)

85

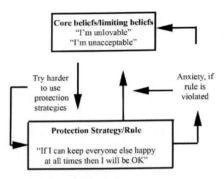

Figure 4. Limiting belief pathway.

Let's hypothesise that you have a limiting belief "I'm not a nice person" and the protection strategy is that, if I keep everyone else happy at all times, then I'll be OK."

"OK. What behaviours might be used to keep your protection strategy in place?"

Client: "Well, maybe to go with the flow ...

86

Avoid conflict as much as possible ... Do things that I don't really want to do to keep others happy ... Maybe put a happy front on ..."

Therapist: "OK. How might others react to you when you do that?"

Client: "I suppose they're fine with it."

Therapist: "And what about when somebody asks you to do something that you don't agree with, or that you don't want to do?"

Client: "I may end up going along with it, I suppose ..."

Therapist: "And how do you feel when you go along with things that you really don't want to?"

Client: "Resentful, angry, frustrated ..."

Therapist: "So how does that show itself?"

Client: "I suppose I get more withdrawn."

Therapist: "So how do other people react to you when you become withdrawn?"

Client: "They keep trying to find out what's wrong."

Therapist: "So what do you tell them?"
Client: "Nothing ..."

Therapist: "And when you do that how do others react?"

Client: "I guess they get frustrated and angry with me."

Therapist: "So what do you do then?"

Client: "I suppose ... I become even more withdrawn."

Therapist: "So how do others react then?"

Client: "I guess there's a general sense of tension."

Therapist: "And when that's going on, how happy are others around you?"

Client: "No one's happy."

Therapist: "So when this is going on, how much do you feel you're lovable and acceptable?"

Client: "Not very much."

Therapist: "So how effective are your protection strategies really?"

Client: "It seems stupid when you think about it like that ... And, when it's drawn out in black and white, it seems so obvious! So why haven't I seen this before?"

Therapist: "Well, when the wheel was

invented do you think people asked
themselves that same question?"

Client: "I guess it seems obvious after-
wards. But it feels very different when
you're in it!"

Therapist: "Yes it does – And the important thing to recognise now is that you
have the beginning of awareness of what is
happening. Once you have awareness, it's
important to think about gradually
starting to drop your maladaptive
protection strategies and, once you've
started to drop them, to assess what
actually happens. For example, if you tell
somebody that you can't do something, or
you have to let somebody down, although
the other person may feel disappointed,
will he or she really think that you're not a
nice person and reject you from that point
onwards?"

Session 16

Unlocking Maladaptive Protection Strategies

"It is very important to take some time to work out the kinds of things that you do to protect yourself from your limiting beliefs and, following that to assess how effective your protection strategies really are."

Client: "But, I don't understand why my brain would develop these maladaptive protection strategies initially.

Therapist: "Well, let's go back to the five-year-old boy that we talked about in Session 12. Now we know that the boy did what he needed to do to get some positive attention. From an evolutionary point of view, it's very adaptive for us as children to do what's necessary to bond with our main carers, because ostensibly, if we don't bond, our survival may be at stake. It's this fundamental human need for attachment that creates the fabric for the rules or protection strategies. What I'm really wanting to repeat here is that the rules start off as an adaptive way of dealing with a *mal*adaptive environment but, as time goes on and the environment changes to a more adaptive environment, the rules become maladaptive."

Client: "So why doesn't my brain just automatically change the rules when the environment changes?"

Therapist: "Now you've really found the crux of the problem. Often, when a brain successfully works out a way of doing something well, it doesn't automatically revise and review. Instead it continues to keep using the same process even when it's outdated or doesn't work anymore. Sometimes, when it doesn't work, the brain can tend to do it even more, thinking that it will eventually work. Have you ever seen a fly on a window pane, continually smacking into the glass, trying to get free, when all along there's an opening in the window just centimetres away."

Client: "So how do I get my brain to change the rules?"

Therapist: "To do this, we need to bring the rules into our consciousness – to become aware of what we are doing and decide to change! Then, following this, consider how the changes have worked. If we consciously repeat an alternative strategy, for example putting our own needs first rather than trying to keep others happy, while at the same time continuing to reflecting on what we're doing, and about what happens when we behave differently, our brain very soon starts to develop new automatic processes."

Client: "After our previous session (you may think that this is strange, but) although I know that my maladaptive protection strategies don't work and I know that attempting to keep people happy at all times doesn't work – I still find myself compelled to go along with the idea. Is it just because I'm used to doing things the old way? Will I ever be able to change?"

Therapist: "Let's remember that if you drop a protection strategy, for example attempting to keep others happy at all times, it's likely that you'll feel highly anxious. This is because you'll be making a connection with one of your limiting beliefs, for example, "I'm not a nice person". When this happens, part of you will be frightened about what could happen to you – maybe you think the past will repeat itself. Maybe you think people will react negatively to you."

"In fact, you don't really know what's going to happen until you do it. When we're in this situation all we can do is embrace the fear and continue consciously to change our behaviour. Think of it like an experiment, in which you're a scientist making subtle changes simply to see what happens or to watch how others react. When we no longer believe that there's something wrong with us or that we're bad in some way there's nothing to defend or protect ourselves from. We're free, quite simply, to be ourselves."

Session 17

Using the Law of Opposites

"A useful rule of thumb when dealing with depressed mood is to think: what could I do to make myself feel worse? Make a list, and make your list as exhaustive as possible. When your list is complete, take each point on the list and write down exactly what you would need to do to make it happen.
Then do the opposite!"

Client: "I'm slightly frightened of doing this. I feel as though I've come a long way and if I start thinking about what might make me feel worse, I'll get depressed again."

Therapist: "Well, I can understand why you'd think that. However, in order to truly reduce the risk of relapsing into old ways of being, we need to be aware of the risk factors. When you're able to do this you'll feel as though you're much more in charge of your life. Now, what things could you think or do to make yourself feel worse?"

Client: "I guess I could isolate myself, stop spending time with others, think that there's something wrong with me, continually ask myself why I'm feeling the way that I do. I could ruminate, dwell on negative issues, think about the worst case scenario or tell myself off. I could think in alls, nothings and everythings – and do all of those things automatically without bringing any of it into my awareness."

Therapist: "That's an impressive list. Now, what I'd like us to do is simply think about one of the factors and then, when we've worked on that, I'd like you to try the same process on the rest of your list by yourself."

Client: "OK. I'll pick the first – Isolating myself."

Therapist: "Right, OK, so what would you need to do to make that happen?"

Client: "I suppose I'd need to stop contacting my friends and acquaintances, when people phone make excuses 162 about why I can't go out, don't phone people back, spend more time on my own or spend a lot of time sleeping."

Therapist: "And what would you need to do to make that happen, for example, how would you need to think?"

Client: "I guess I'd need to convince myself that people would have a better time without me – Tell myself that I'm too tired, tell myself that they don't really want me there."

Therapist: "OK. Now, if you were to do those things what would happen?"

Client: "I suppose I'd become more withdrawn, people would contact me less, then I could somehow turn it around to being about me – I could tell myself that this always happens to me."

Therapist: "How would you feel then?"

Client: "Lonely and isolated."

Therapist: "So I guess the strategy would work then?"

Client: "It seems so obvious when I talk about it."

Therapist: "So we know what the problem will be if you isolate yourself using the strategies that you've just described. ... So what's your solution?"

Client: "Go out more."

Therapist: "And, what will you need to do to make that happen?

Client: Contact people. Look in the local

papers to find out what's happening. Believe that people do enjoy my company. Generally spend more time being with others."

Therapist: "And, when you do those things, what will be the outcome?"

Client: "I'd probably have less time to worry about feeling low. I'd just feel a lot better."

Therapist: "Now the important thing to do is to work through the rest of your list using the same procedure – And I predict that what you'll discover is that it boils down to a simple choice. Engage in old types of thinking and behaviour and you'll have predictable and recognisable negative results. Engage in *alternative* types of thinking and behaviour and you'll get different, more positive results. The new results will be highly preferable not only because you'll be living a life you value, but also because you'll be feeling well."

100

"Remember, remember, remember – The law of opposites."

Session 18

Now Choose to Know

"Knowledge of how we can make things better in our lives can, at times, cause us to come into conflict with others. Sometimes this conflict influences us to make a choice. At this time we can either forget what we know, or we can use what we know. Having knowledge is not the same as using the knowledge we have. When we choose to know, we are actively and deliberately using our knowledge."

Client: "That seems very cryptic! How can people forget what they know?"

Therapist: "I'll explain. Throughout our sessions I've offered you ideas and strategies to help you feel better about yourself. Using these strategies on a regular basis will influence you to take charge of your life and improve your mood. However, I've found that some people can gradually stop using their strategies and revert back to their original negative position."

Client: "I don't understand! Why would I stop using the strategies when I know I could revert back?"

Therapist: "Well, it doesn't always work consciously. At times, other people in our environment may pull us back into old ways of doing things. We might simply choose not to remember what we've learnt."

Client: "But, I don't understand why other people would pull me back, when it makes me depressed."

Therapist: "They don't do it deliberately – It's just that sometimes other people can obtain subtle benefits from you doing things the old way, for example you pleasing them at all times, and suchlike."

Client: "I see that."

Therapist: "Think of yourself like a harp that has just been tuned after being left for 30 years. If the harp is then left without further retuning it will rapidly go out of tune, because the strings have such a long history of being in specific positions. So directly after the harp has been tuned, the strings will quickly start reverting back to their original positions. Add to this the impact of others who may be subtly loosening or tightening the strings to suit their own purposes."

Client: "So what do I do?"

Therapist: "It's quite simple, you need to tune the harp on a regular basis, and eventually you'll train the strings to stay in the positions that you want them to be in. Your tuning equipment will be your cognitive and behavioural strategies covered in our sessions so far. These strategies will need to be used regularly and on a daily basis. It's not dissimilar to cleaning your teeth. I'm pretty sure that most of us don't clean our teeth every now and again or even just once. We clean them every day."

"What I'm inviting you to do is to choose to remember and to use these strategies, rather than simply owning them and putting them to one side. Essentially, what I'm suggesting here is that you can choose to know!"

Conclusion

Hopefully, now you have read this book, you are aware that what you do and think right now dictates your future and how it will unfold.

Few of us actually focus on each new, unique second. We are, instead, in the past, so to speak. So it will be the past, its prejudices and experiences that predict and dictate our future and not this moment right now.

The good news is that all of us have the potential to live from right now. This is not to deny our past experiences, but it is to deny the potential continued negative impact of the past on our present and therefore on our future. We have no control of what has passed. We have control of only right now.

The most important relationship any of us have is with our body and with our mind. How we relate to ourselves affects every other relationship around us. While we do not have actual control over others and how they behave towards us, we do have choice and control over how we behave towards ourselves. How we relate to ourselves can directly affect how others relate to us.

Fortunately, we have the ability to think about our thinking. This means that we do not have to be bound by the mind's content and our automatic responses. Choosing to have awareness without judgement is the magic we can use to liberate us from past prejudices, learnings and conditioning that otherwise keep us stuck, preventing us moving forward in life as we would like to.

Index

Glossary

Acceptance – Process of welcoming uncomfortable sensations.

Adaptive environment – An environment that helps an individual to flourish.

Attention Deficit Disorder – A medical term used to describe poor ability to hold attention.

Black and white thinking – Polarized thinking e.g. things are either good or bad, there is no in between.

Cognitive – A word commonly used by psychologists to describe a mental process.

Cognitive Behaviour Therapy (CBT) – A therapy that helps individuals to improve their mood by altering the way that they think and behave.

Cognitive feedback loop – Process where information is moved from one part of the brain to another and back again.

Compensate – A psychological term used to describe behaviours that we use to protect ourselves from feared painful beliefs.

Conscious awareness – A term often used to indicate that an individual is aware of his or her own thinking processes.

Coping strategies – Problem solving strategies that we often use to minimise our distress.

Depression – Persistent and enduring low mood, usually accompanied by poor concentration, interest, memory, sleep, appetite, motivation, energy, and libido.

Distorted thinking patterns – Used to describe thinking processes that filter, alter or block information to such a degree that an individual gains access to only a fraction of the information potentially available.

Egocentric – A belief that things arise or are centred around the existence of the self. Often related to children believing that things happen directly because of them.

Hypothesis – Possible explanation based on the information available.

Limiting beliefs – Beliefs about the self which can lead to restricted thinking styles, defensive behaviours, and emotional upset.

Maladaptive environment – An environment that prevents an individual from thriving, growing or developing.

Maladaptive protection strategies – Defensive thoughts and behaviours that create the illusion of safety.

Perception – Often automatic, this is the end product of a filtering process that our brain uses to organise information that comes into sensory awareness.

Physiological reaction – Changes that occur within the body in response to a triggering event.

Protection strategies – Ways of thinking and/or behaving that we use to defend ourselves from painful emotions.

Reinforcement of beliefs – Ways of thinking, feeling or behaving that tend provide evidence for what we believe.

Reflection – Thinking about our thinking or behaviour.

Rules – Ideas or expectations that we hold that are often connected to how we think others should think, feel or behave.

Rumination – A process of churning thoughts over and over within one's mind.

Suppression – An act of pushing down painful feelings.

Thinking style – A pattern of thinking that often occurs automatically.

Trigger – A term often used by therapists to describe an event (e.g., break-up of a relationship) that may have increased the chance of a mental health problem developing.

Visualise – A process of holding imaginary thoughts (e.g., images, sounds etc.) in our mind.

Working hypothesis - A hypothesis that is subjected to continuous change as increased information becomes available.

Common medications

Alprazolam – A benzodiazepine prescribed for panic, generalised anxiety, phobias, social anxiety, and OCD.

Amitriptyline – A tricyclic antidepressant.

Atenolol – A beta-blocker prescribed for anxiety.

Buspirone – A mild tranquiliser prescribed for generalised anxiety, OCD and panic.

Chlordiazepoxide – A benzodiazepine prescribed for generalised anxiety, and phobias.

Citalopram – A selective serotonin reuptake inhibitor commonly prescribed for mixed anxiety and depression.

Clomipramine – A tricyclic antidepressant.

Clonazepam – A benzodiazepine prescribed for panic, generalised anxiety, phobias, and social anxiety.

Desipramine – A tricyclic anti-depressant.

Diazepam – A benzodiazepine prescribed for generalised anxiety, panic, and phobias.

Doxepin – A tricyclic antidepressant.

Duloxetine – A serotonin-norepinephrine reuptake inhibitor.

Escitalopram Oxalate – A selective serotonin reuptake inhibitor.

Fluoxetine - A selective serotonin reuptake inhibitor.

Fluvoxamine – A selective serotonin reuptake inhibitor.

Gabapentin – An anticonvulsant prescribed for generalised anxiety and social anxiety.

Imipramine – A tri-cyclic antidepressant.

Lorazepam – A benzodiazepine prescribed for generalised anxiety, panic and phobias.

Nortriptyline – A tricyclic antidepressant.

Oxazepam – A benzodiazepine prescribed for generalised anxiety and phobias.

Paroxetine – A selective serotonin reuptake inhibitor.

Phenelzine – A monoamine oxidase inhibitor.

Pregabalin – An anticonvulsant prescribed for generalised anxiety disorder.

Propanalol – A beta blocker prescribed for anxiety.

Sertraline - A selective serotonin reuptake inhibitor.

Tranylcypromine – A monoamine oxidase inhibitor.

Valproate – An anticonvulsant prescribed for panic.

Venlafaxine – A serotonin-norepinephrine reuptake inhibitor.

Printed in Great Britain
by Amazon